National Library of Australia Cataloguing-in-Publication:
Creator: Cahill, Jennifer, author.
Title: Flip charting quick guide and handy hints / Jennifer Cahill.
ISBN: 9780994456106 (paperback)
ISBN: 9780994456113 (ebook)
Subjects: Business presentations.
                  Business communication.
                  Charts, diagrams, etc.
Dewey Number: 658.452

Cover Design: Pickawoowoo Publishing Group

Publisher: Jennifer Cahill trading as Inspired Clarity
                 PO Box 156, Scarborough QLD 4020
                 www.jennifercahill.com.au

Welcome to

FLIP CHARTING

Quick Guide
and
Handy Hints

by Jennifer Cahill

Contents

Hi!

Welcome to Flip Chart Quick Guide and Handy Hints.

This book has been developed as an introduction to flip charting and is a quick reference guide of handy hints on how to get started.

Creating flip charts became an integral part of my own career in facilitation. I was often asked to run sessions for new presenters, trainers and managers on how to create effective flip charts.

This book is a snap shot of some of the key elements involved in creating flip charts. It has been designed to be simple and easy to follow, so that anyone seeking dynamic and engaging presentation methods can pick it up and run with it.

Inspire your creativity and further engage your learners through the art of flip charting.

Thank you to everyone that I have trained, as you have been instrumental in bringing this tool to life!

Reference this book when you are seeking inspiration, tips and techniques for your next presentation…..

….unleash your full creative potential!

1

Imagine...

- You are sitting in a meeting room with your colleagues.
- Together, you are about to experience multiple electronic presentations. These are full of important information that you will be required to integrate into your role. So you know you need to pay attention!
- You are ready, waiting and prepared to watch slide show....after slide show....after slide show. You've been here before.
- While the first presenter is organising the technology, you chat idly with the person next to you as you wait.
- It starts............click...............move forward a slide...........

  ....click..........move to the next slide............

  ....click........click.......click.......zzzzzzz

- The presentations start to morph together.....click.......click......
- You mind starts to wander......
- You ask yourself, "When will this presentation end?"
- "I know there is important information in there somewhere"

  .....click.....click......click....yawn........

- You take a sip of your drink and attempt to jot down a few notes on the page in front of you.
- You are trying your hardest to remain focused.
- Finally, the presentation comes to an end.
- You take a deep breath as you turn to a fresh page in your note book.
- You start to brace yourself for the next presentation to start.

- As the fifth presentation starts, you become aware that no one is moving around setting up technology.
- You notice that there is no electronic presentation!
- The presenter steps up to the front. They have a marker in their hand.
- Your eyes light up as the presentation begins. What is it that they are doing?
- They are writing on a flip chart!

You become curious.

You are engaged!

- With bright colours and sketches, key messages are being highlighted on the chart.

Your imagination is captured.

You are involved!

- The presenter has put the flip charts on the walls all around the room. You are immersed in the flip charts.
- All the presentations have now been completed.
- The previous electronic presentations have long disappeared into cyber space and have all but disappeared from your memory.
- The colourful, engaging flip charts remain on the walls around you. You are drawn to the colours and images on the charts. You take a moment to reflect and review the key messages that have been skilfully portrayed.

Flip Charting will be great for my presentation because...

Use this page to capture your thoughts on *why* and *how* Flip Charting could be a dynamic option for your next presentation. Think about what it would mean for you as well as your audience.

Why Flip Chart Anyway?

Boost your presentation!

- Our brains get bored seeing similar mediums being used.

- Change it up! Surprise people in your next presentation!

- Inspire learning and thinking.

Appeal to "Visual" type learners!

- Flip charts will aid learners that need to "see" what you are talking about.

Create content credibility!

- Using Flip Charts creates an air of credibility.

- They demonstrate preparation, passion and real care about the content you are presenting.

Stay in Control!

- Flip Charts can help you stay on track with timing.

- As you have planned or pre-prepared your Flip Charts, you will feel more in control of your presentation.

- You will know where your presentation is headed to next.

When people see the effort you have made, they will care more about their own learning. Plus....it is way more FUN!

People will be engaged and retain more information from your presentation!!!

My Checklist of Tools

I have prepared the following tools for my presentation.

☐ Notebook
☐ Flip Chart Paper
☐ Flip chart stand
☐ Coloured Markers
☐ Tack
☐ Pencil
☐ Ruler
☐ Eraser
☐ Stencils

Extra resources and tools I will need are:

☐ _____
☐ _____
☐ _____
☐ _____
☐ _____
☐ _____

Tools You Will Need

● FLIP CHART PAPER

- Also known as butcher paper.

- Flip Chart paper needs to be of good quality so the markers do not transfer to the sheets underneath.

- The size of the paper you use depends on what you are training and how big your group is.

● FLIP CHART STAND

- There are lots on the market! Even portable "A" frame Flip Charts!

- Make sure it is the right height for you.

- Look for stands that can be moved (on wheels) and ones that have a pen holder at the base.

● COLOURED MARKERS

- Use colour! As many colours as you can find!

- Chiselled markers are the best as you can get different widths as you write, adding more variety to your charts.

- By the way....whiteboard markers are for whiteboards! These do not work smoothly on Flip Chart paper.

- Renew your markers often as they can wear and fray after multiple uses.

● EXTRA ITEMS

- Get yourself a notebook, pencil, eraser and ruler!

- Tack is great for hanging completed charts around the room as opposed to tape, which has been known to peel paint from walls.

Getting Started

PLAN

- It's all in your planning.
- Use a notebook to plan in first.
- Storyboard your flipcharts.

In your notebook:

- Write down a heading for each chart.
- Write key points under each heading.
- Be selective with the points you will add to each chart – keep it simple, as less is more.
- Sketch what you want each flipchart to look like – this makes creating your charts easier as you have planned it!

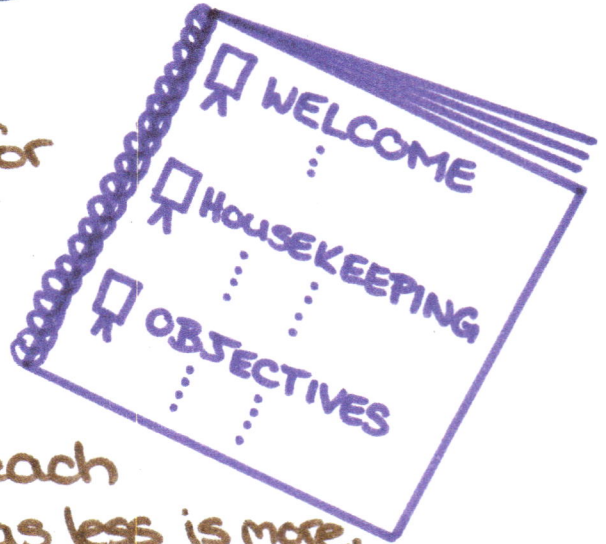

WELCOME

HOUSEKEEPING

OBJECTIVES

Practice

- The more you practice, the easier it becomes.

- Use whiteboards to practice.
- Plan each flipchart.
- Own your flipcharts ∽ make sure that you create them, as this gives you control and credibility.

Getting Started

- Say less with more.
- Use pictures in place of words.

- Pictures speak a thousand words.
- They inspire creative thinking.
- The less words on your charts, the more impact they will have.

Colours

- Be brave.... Get bold!
- Use a variety of colours to bring your charts to life.

- Did you know that some people see red & green as the same colour?
- When using colour to show differences, "Red and Green can not be seen."
- And as for YELLOW, it's hard to read. Save yellow for highlighting, not writing.

FRAME IT!

FRAME IT!

- Frames complete your charts.
- Frames can indicate new topics.
- Frames can signify important information.
- Frames bring out colours you want to highlight.
- Frames can be fun and creative.

Choosing the BEST colour.

Same image....
....different coloured frames.

.—. Make colours pop!—.

The colour of the frame draws out the same colour in the image, bringing it to the front.

FRAMING with Colour

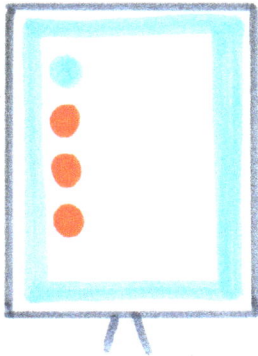

∽ Draw attention to key points. ∽

🔖 Use bullet points or text in the same colour as the frame to make a bold statement.

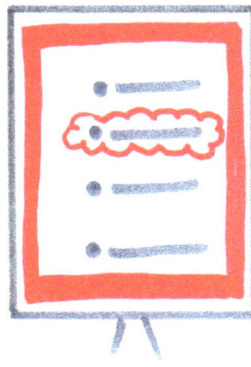

🔖 Highlight important points in the same colour as the frame.
It will help viewers remember it more.

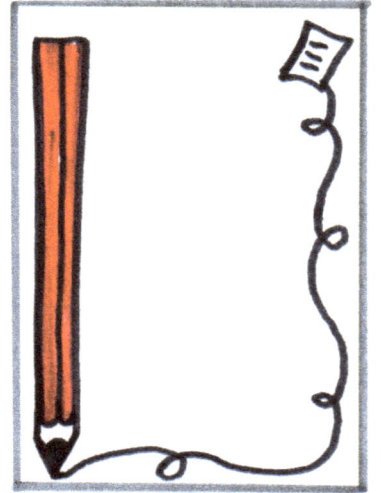

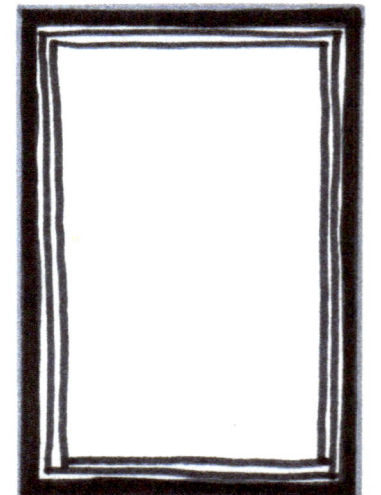

FRAME IDEAS

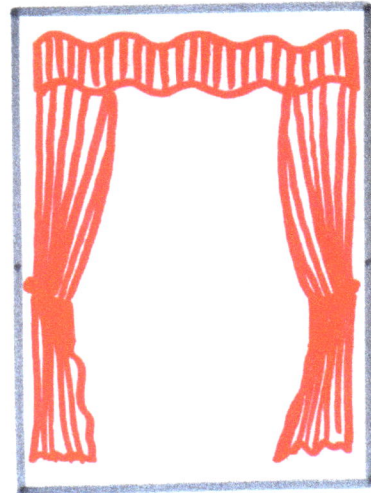

15

MAKE A POINT!

ARROWS

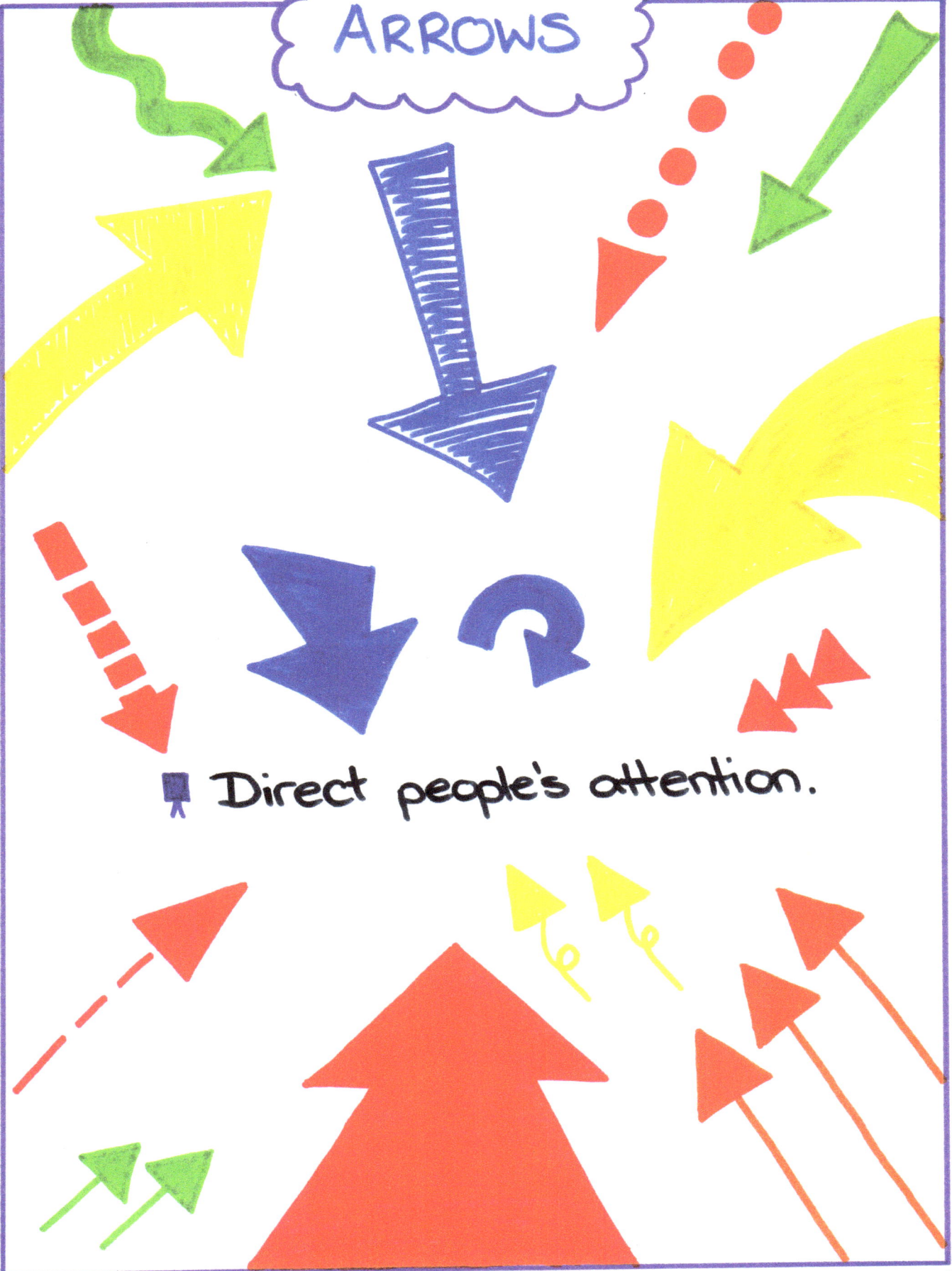

■ Direct people's attention.

MAKE a POINT

- Use large icons to draw attention.
- Centered, in corners or to the side.

Point well made.

Bullet Points

Make a STATEMENT

● BIG or
• small.
● Put them in your FRAMES.

Be creative!

Bold colours.

Use shapes.

19

ICON IDEAS

Use ICONS in place of words.

 Tea

 Coffee

 Lunch

 Lunch

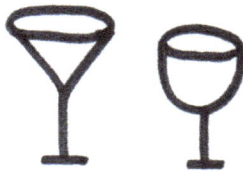 Drinks

 Wine

 Housekeeping

    Books

 Mail

 Cars

 Vans

 Travel

 Planes

 Telephone

 Laptop

 T.V.

 Mobile

🔖 Use colour to bring ICONS to life.

Steps   Tracks   Islands

FLAGS

 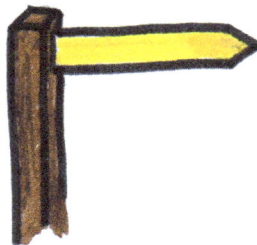 

🔖 Journey ..... distance .....

 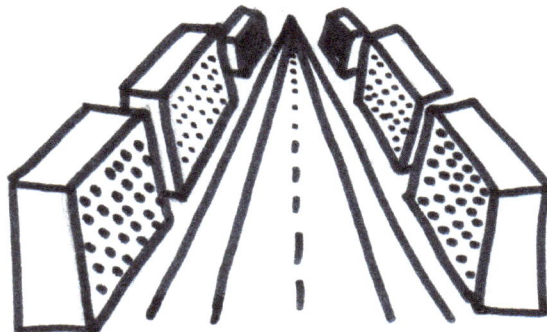

DRAWING IMAGES

DRAWING IMAGES

Use lettering to create simple images.

A B C D E F G H I J K L M

N O P Q R S T U V W X Y Z

a b c d e f g h i j k l m n o p q r s t u v w x y z

   **1.**   **2.**   **3.**   **4.**

FACES

USE:
c n o ɔ ⁄ \

MICE

USE:
∩ ∧ ×

CATS

USE:
o Q M

BIRDS

USE:
S v u ×

DRAWING EYES

Create your own unique faces here!

DRAWING EYES

- Eyes can be used to express emotions.
- Use lines and dots to create eyes.

-- || .. oo

 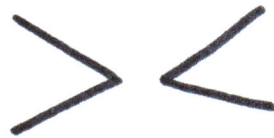

DRAWING NOSES

Create your own unique faces here!

DRAWING NOSES

- Create different faces by changing the shape of the nose.

- Using the same shaped face, changing the nose gives a whole new look.

Nose shapes

DRAWING HAIR

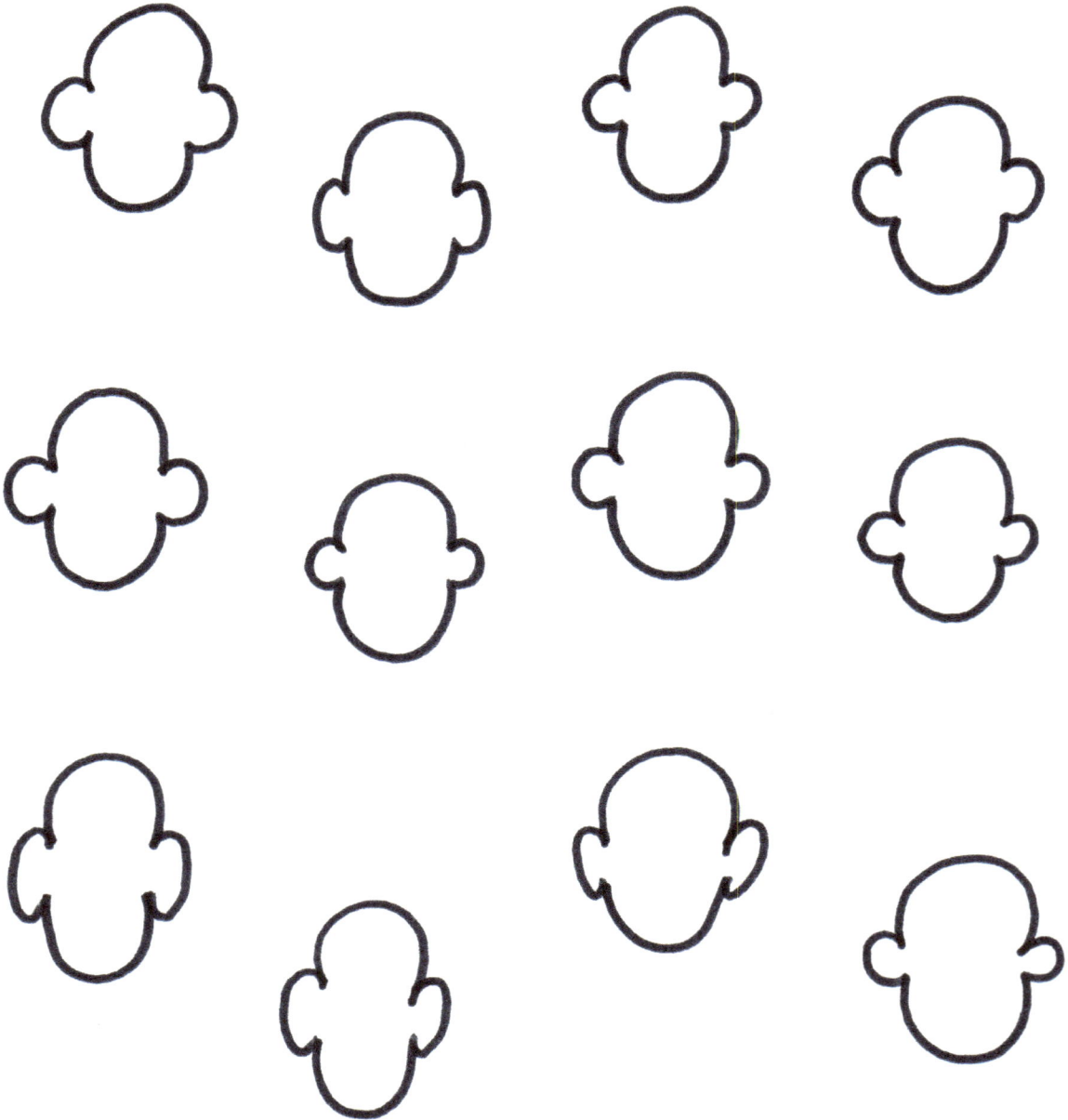

Create your own unique faces here!

Add hair to create more character.

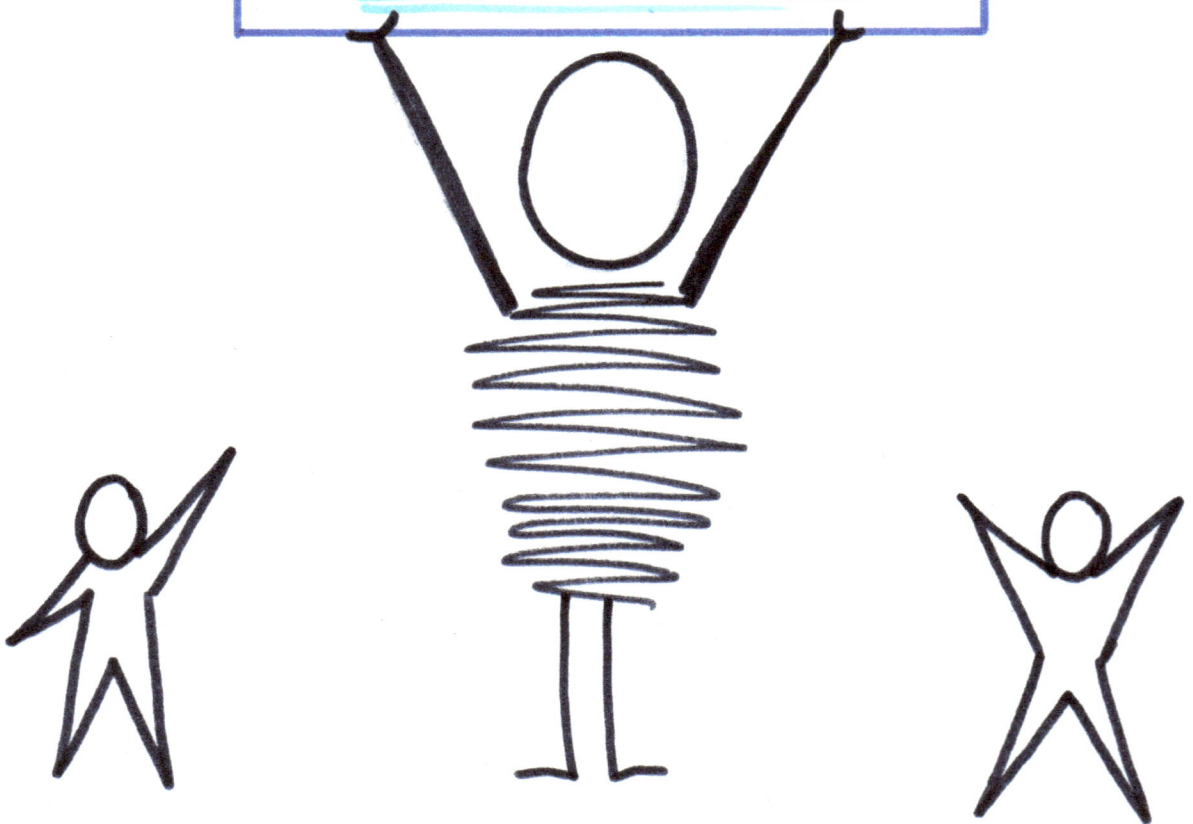

PEOPLE ON THE GO

- Create simple people that add movement and character to charts.
- No faces required, only shapes!

	1.	2.	3.	4.
Enthusiasm				
Action				
Statement				
Pointing				

- Practice on whiteboards first.
- Add people to charts as you present too!

- Get creative!
- Find inspiration in observing body language.

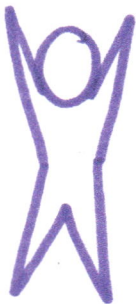

People can hang about ANYWHERE

PEOPLE IN GROUPS

Create groups of people to help engage and involve your audience.

Get creative and have some fun!

Simple to create on the go.

Lettering

Lettering

Lettering

LETTERING

LETTERING

Lettering

34

LETTERING

- Create impact using clear, bold lettering in headings.
- Write in pencil first and use a ruler to keep it straight.

STAND OUT

mIx iTuP to keep audience engaged.

outline ←

GRAB ATTENTION → Write sdrow backwards

Create Lasting Impressions

- Remember to keep text to a minimum on each chart for greater impact.

My Lettering

_____

_____

_____

_____

_____

_____

_____

_____

_____

_____

_____

_____

Use this space to practice lettering!

MY LETTERING

Use this space to practice lettering!

WHERE TO NEXT ?

WHERE TO NEXT

- Tack completed charts to the walls. This will help people retain information.

- Allow reflection time for people to review the charts and embed learning.

- Take photos of your charts and store them for future reference.

- Store charts that can be used again by hanging them, rolling them or lying them flat.

- Continue to have fun creating dynamic and engaging flip charts!

This space is for you to capture images and icons that you have created!

This space is for you to capture images and icons that you have created!

This space is for you to capture images and icons that you have created!

42

This space is for you to capture images and icons that you have created!

About the Author

Jennifer Cahill is an intuitive Life Strategist, coach, facilitator and motivational speaker who guides and empowers people through a journey of self-actualisation to inspire their true potential personally and professionally.

A qualified NLP Practitioner and certified trainer and assessor, Jennifer's remarkable ability to analyse complex situations and identify core elements of problems enables her to structure and deliver unique, specific, practical solutions that create positive change; helping others to achieve their desired individual and business outcomes.

Jennifer has been delivering dynamic training and coaching sessions throughout Australia and overseas for over 15 years. Having experienced multiple diverse cultures, Jennifer has developed a deep appreciation, understanding and respect for personal and business needs.

Her experiences have given her a multidimensional perspective in her approach to connecting with people, creating specific solutions and positive outcomes.

As the founder and owner of *Inspired Clarity*, Jennifer provides intuitive coaching to individuals and businesses through a variety of modalities, creating effective strategies that help clarify and prioritise goals, identifying external and internal challenges that prevent people from reaching their goals as well as assisting people in proactively embracing and enhancing new skill sets.

Jennifer is sort after for her warm, lively and good-humoured approach to her subject matter; her ability to tailor effective training solutions; her dynamic facilitation skills and inspirational speeches.

Discover more at:

www.jennifercahill.com.au

- Subscribe to our free E-Newsletter.
- Purchase books and art work.
- View *Inspired Clarity's* upcoming events.
- Join in discussions through our blog.

Contact us at:

Address: PO Box 156 Scarborough, QLD. 4020.

e-mail: jennifercahill.ic@gmail.com

..............Unleash your fullest potential.

www.ingramcontent.com/pod-product-compliance
Lightning Source LLC
Chambersburg PA
CBHW041101050426
42334CB00063B/3279